Object Rhymes

Pumpkins Everywhere

Reproducible emergent readers to make and take home

By Jean Warren • Illustrated by Barb Tourtillotte

Totline® Publications
A Division of Frank Schaffer Publications, Inc.
Torrance, California

Managing Editor: Kathleen Cubley
Contributing Editors: Gayle Bittinger, Elizabeth McKinnon,
   Susan M. Sexton
Proofreader: Miriam Bulmer
Graphic Design (Interior): Kathy Kotomaimoce
Layout Artist: Gordon Frazier, Sarah Ness
Graphic Design (Cover): Brenda Mann Harrison
Editorial Assistant: Durby Peterson
Production Manager: Melody Olney

Formerly published by Totline® Publications as
Totline "Take-Home" Books—Object Rhymes.

ISBN 1-57029-278-7

Library of Congress Catalog Card Number 98-61313

Printed in the United States of America
Published by Totline® Publications

Business Office: 23740 Hawthorne Blvd.
   Torrance, CA 90505

Introduction

Young children who are just becoming interested in books and reading are usually long on enthusiasm and short on ability. Totline® Reproducible Rhyme Books are designed to capture that enthusiasm.

Each of the beginning emergent readers in *Object Rhymes* reinforces beginning alphabet concepts and is written in repetitive rhyme. The unique feature of these rhymes is that young children are able to "read" them, using the pictures as their guides. This happens because each rhyme is simply written and illustrated with beginning readers in mind. After reading a book with an adult a few times, your children will be able to read it by themselves.

All of the books in this series are reproducible, so each child can have his or her own copy. Watch your students glow with pride and a feeling of accomplishment as they take home their own books to "read" to their families.

Pumpkins by the table.

Pumpkins by the chair.

Pumpkins by the door.

Pumpkins everywhere!

Contents

Fall Books

Winter Books

Spring Books

Summer Books

The page numbers listed above are on the inside margins of each page.

How to Use Totline®
Reproducible Rhyme Books

1. Tear out the pages for the book of your choice.

2. For double-sided copies, copy the odd-numbered pages on the front of the paper and the appropriate even-numbered pages on the back, and then cut the pages in half. For single-sided copies, simply copy the pages and cut them in half.

3. Give each child two 5½-by-8-inch pieces of construction paper to use for book covers. Let the children decorate their books covers as desired or use one of the suggestions listed below.

4. If desired, place the book pages on a table and let the children help collate them into books. (Younger children may need help with this process.)

5. Help the children bind their books using a stapler or a hole punch and paper fasteners.

Cover Decorating Ideas

1. Let the children use rubber stamps or stickers that correspond to the rhyme's subject to decorate the covers of the books.

2. Cut sponges into appropriate shapes. Let the children use the sponges like stamps to print designs on their book covers.

3. Make paint pads by folding paper towels, placing them in shallow containers, and pouring small amounts of tempera paint on them. Give the children cookie cutters in the appropriate shapes. Have them dip their cookie cutters into the paint and then press them on the covers of their books.

5. Let the children cut out and glue appropriate magazine pictures on their book covers.

6. Have the children write their names on the backs of their books.

Extended Learning Ideas

1. Enlarge the pages of a book on a photocopier to make a big book. Let the children color the illustrations on the pages.

2. Incorporate the books into a larger seasonal theme unit.

3. Let your children find and color the main object in a story. Then, have them color the rest of the pictures.

4. Add lines for writing to the bottom of each of the pages of a story (see example below). On the writing lines, use dotted lines to print the name of the object the theme object is "on." For example, print the word "flowers" if the story says "Butterflies on the flowers." Photocopy a classroom set of the story. Let your children trace over the printed word on each page.

Turkeys by the pumpkins. 1

Turkeys by the haystack.

p 20 © 1998 Totline® Publications

2 **Turkeys by the well.**

p 20 © 1998 Totline® Publications

Turkeys by the bell.

Turkeys by the barn.

5

Turkeys by the wagon.

7

6   **Turkeys by the corn.**

8   **Turkeys by the horn.**

Turkeys by the wheel.

9

Turkeys by the table.

11

10   **Turkeys by the chair.**

12   **Turkeys everywhere!**

Bows on the bear. 1

Bows on the bed. 3

p 26 © 1998 Totline® Publications

2   **Bows on the doll.**

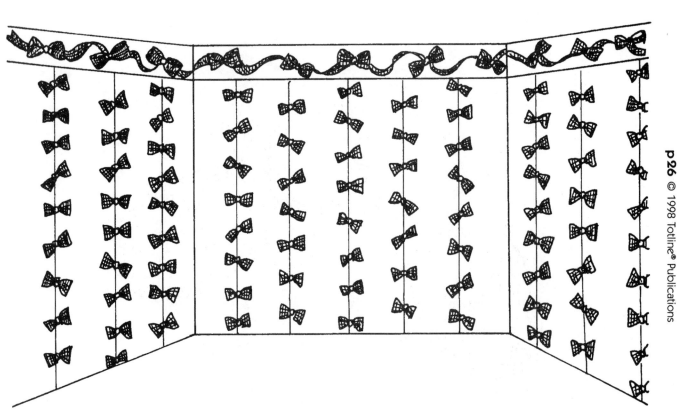

p 26 © 1998 Totline® Publications

4   **Bows on the wall.**

Bows on the dress. 5

Bows on the shoes. 7

6   **Bows on the socks.**

8   **Bows on the box.**

Bows on the candles.

9

Bows on the door.

11

p30 © 1998 Totline® Publications

10   **Bows on the stairs.**

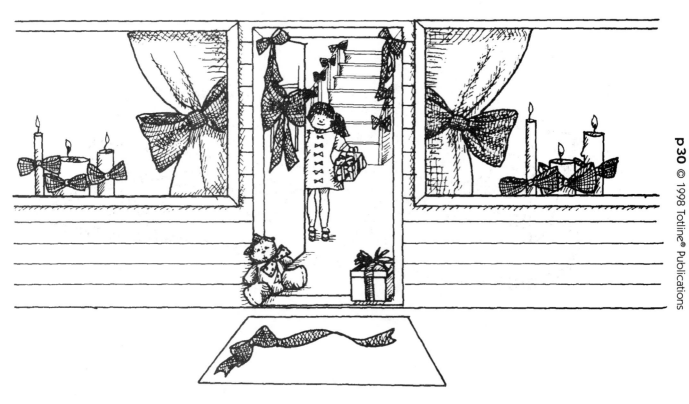

p30 © 1998 Totline® Publications

12   **Bows everywhere!**

Snow on the hill. 1

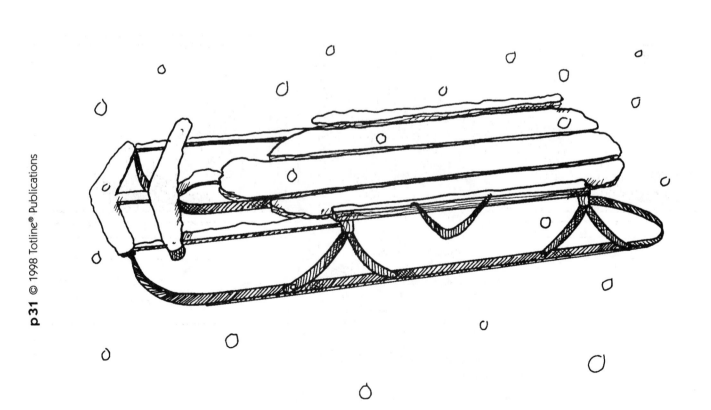

Snow on the sled. 3

2 **Snow on the tree.**

p32 © 1998 Totline® Publications

4 **Snow on me.**

p32 © 1998 Totline® Publications

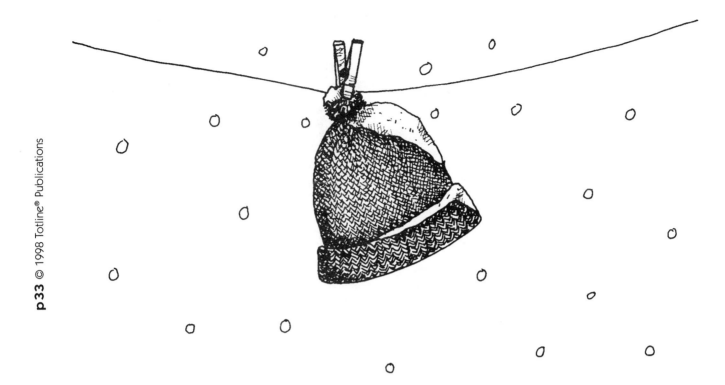

Snow on the hat.

5

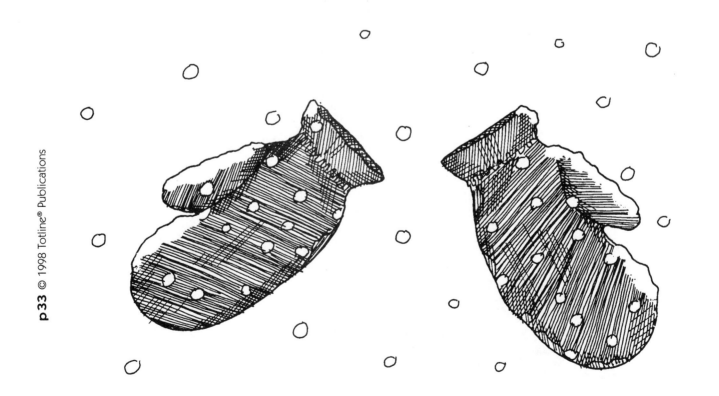

Snow on the mittens.

7

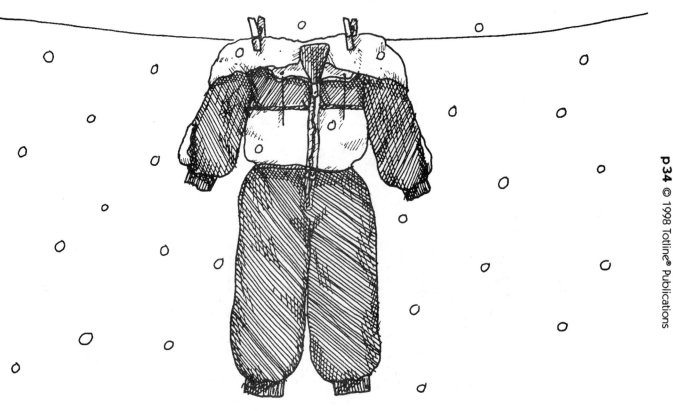

6 **Snow on the suit.**

8 **Snow on the boot.**

Snow on the house.

9

Snow on the window.

11

10   **Snow on the stairs.**

12   **Snow everywhere!**

Hearts on the mailbox. 1

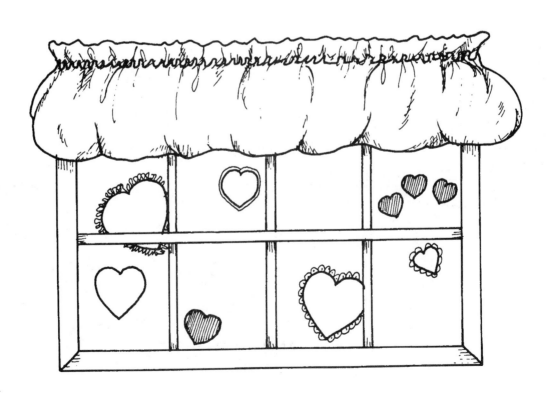

Hearts on the window. 3

2 **Hearts on the door.**

4 **Hearts on the floor.**

Hearts on the cake.

5

Hearts on the shoes.

7

6   **Hearts on the box.**

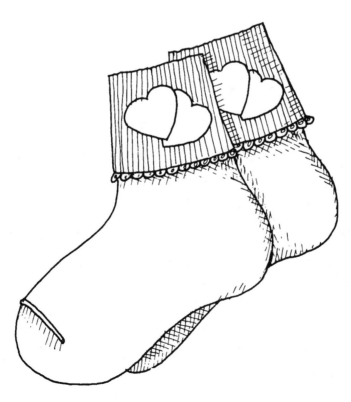

8   **Hearts on the socks.**

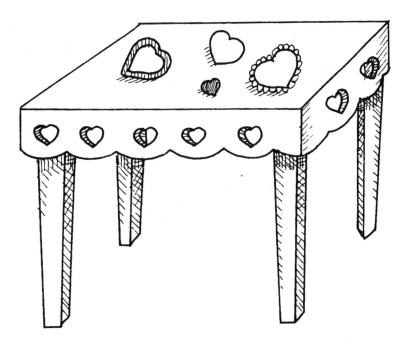

Hearts on the table.

9

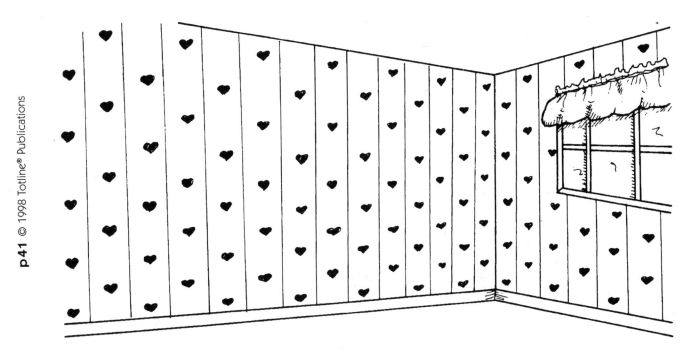

Hearts on the wall.

11

p42 © 1998 Totline® Publications

10 **Hearts on the chair.**

p42 © 1998 Totline® Publications

12 **Hearts everywhere!**

Shamrocks on the coat. 1

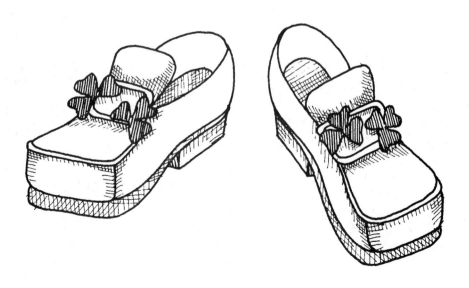

Shamrocks on the shoes. 3

2   **Shamrocks on the hat.**

4   **Shamrocks on the cat.**

Shamrocks on the window.

Shamrocks on the walls.

6 **Shamrocks on the door.**

8 **Shamrocks on the floor.**

Shamrocks on the tables.   9

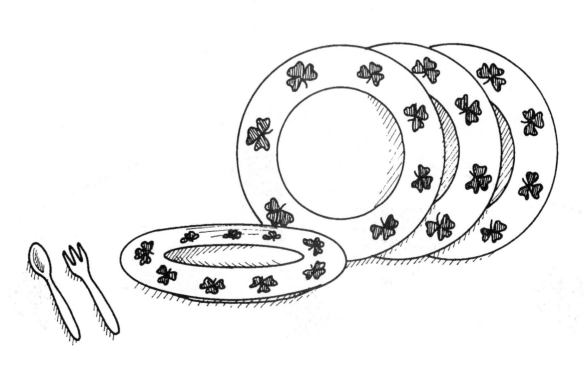

Shamrocks on the plates.   11

p48 © 1998 Totline® Publications

10 **Shamrocks on the chair.**

p48 © 1998 Totline® Publications

12 **Shamrocks everywhere!**

Rain on the cat. 1

Rain on the pigs. 3

p50 © 1998 Totline® Publications

2   **Rain on the dog.**

p50 © 1998 Totline® Publications

4   **Rain on the frog.**

Rain on the barn.

5

Rain on the farmer.

7

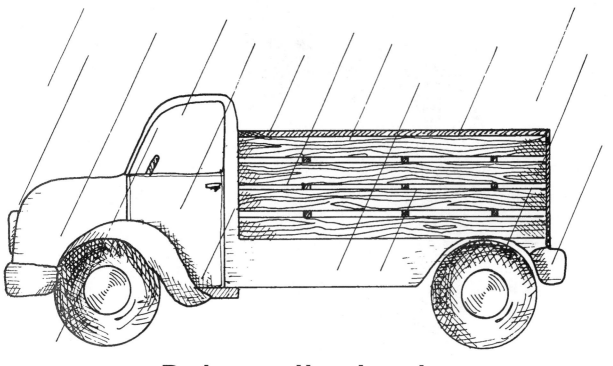

6 **Rain on the truck.**

8 **Rain on the duck.**

Rain on the colt.

9

Rain on the fence.

11

10 **Rain on the mare.**

p54 © 1998 Totline® Publications

12 **Rain everywhere.**

p54 © 1998 Totline® Publications

Flowers on the curtains.

1

Flowers on the pillows.

3

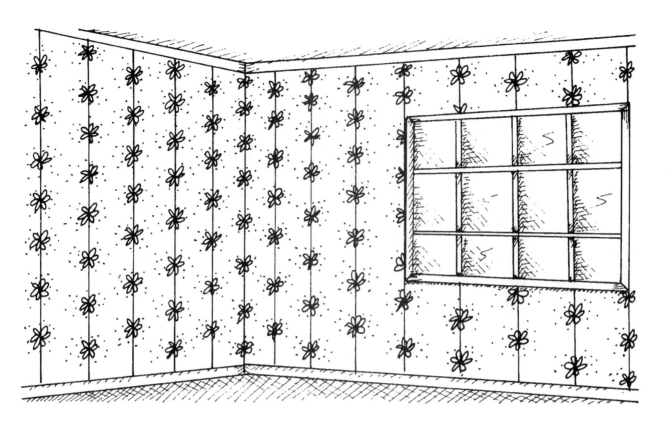

2   **Flowers on the wall.**

p56 © 1998 Totline® Publications

4   **Flowers on the doll.**

p56 © 1998 Totline® Publications

Flowers on the towel.　　　　　**5**

Flowers on the dress.　　　　　**7**

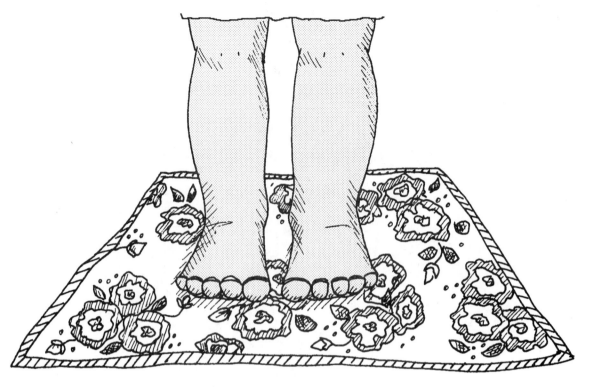

6   **Flowers on the mat.**

p58 © 1998 Totline® Publications

8   **Flowers on the hat.**

p58 © 1998 Totline® Publications

Flowers on the table.

9

Flowers on the cup.

11

10   **Flowers on the chair.**

12   **Flowers everywhere!**

Butterflies on the wagon.

1

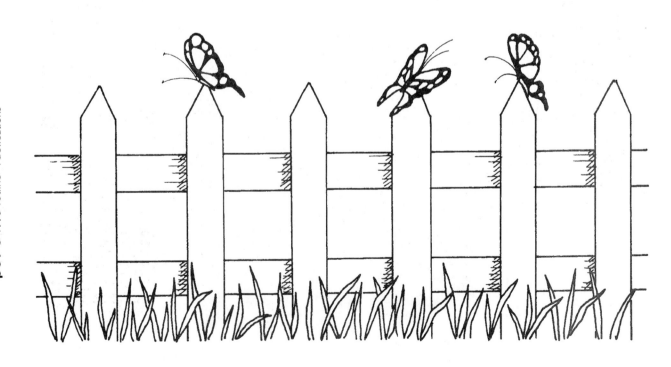

Butterflies on the fence.

3

p62 © 1998 Totline® Publications

2   **Butterflies on the ball.**

p62 © 1998 Totline® Publications

4   **Butterflies on the doll.**

Butterflies on the flowers.

5

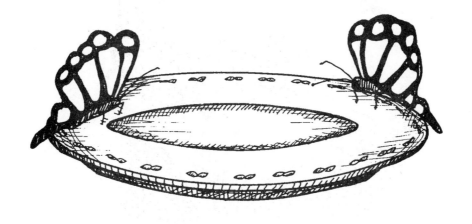

Butterflies on the plate.

7

6 **Butterflies on the grass.**

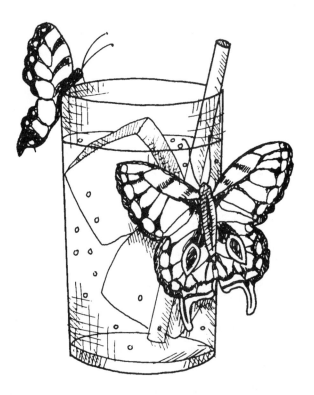

8 **Butterflies on the glass.**

Butterflies on the table.

9

Butterflies on the umbrella.

11

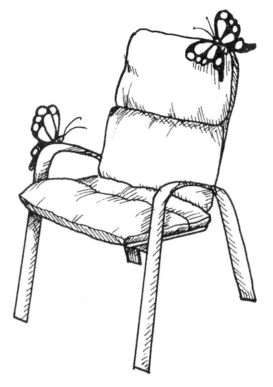

p66 © 1998 Totline® Publications

10 **Butterflies on the chair.**

p66 © 1998 Totline® Publications

12 **Butterflies everywhere!**

Flags on the cars. 1

Flags on the wagons. 3

2   **Flags on the bikes.**

p68 © 1998 Totline® Publications

4   **Flags on the trikes.**

p68 © 1998 Totline® Publications

Flags on the horses. 5

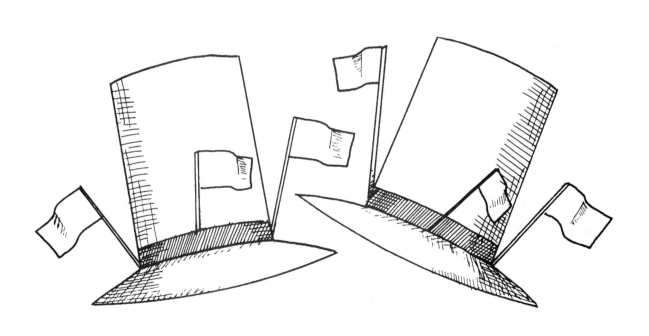

Flags on the hats. 7

6 **Flags on the floats.**

8 **Flags on the coats.**

Flags on the drummers.

9

Flags on the clowns.

11

10 **Flags on the bear.**

12 **Flags everywhere!**

Sand on the beach.

1

Sand on the book.

3

2   **Sand on the doll.**

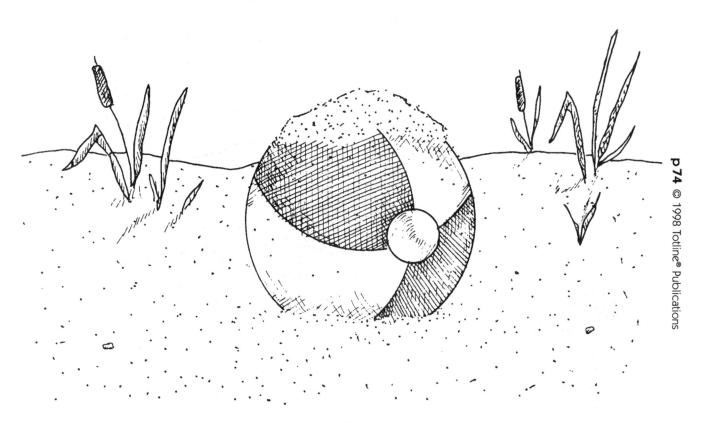

4   **Sand on the ball.**

Sand on the pail.

5

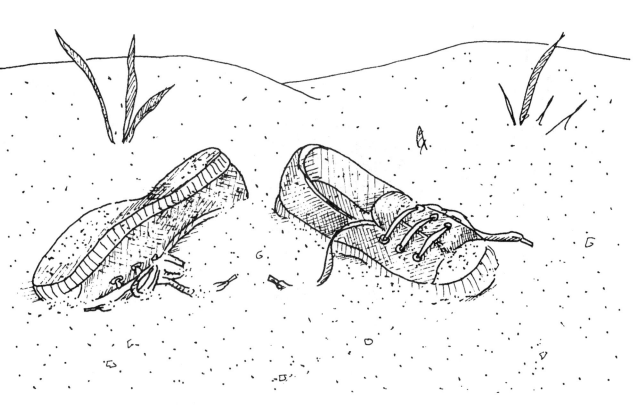

Sand on the shoes.

7

6   **Sand on the box.**

p76 © 1998 Totline® Publications

8   **Sand on the socks.**

p76 © 1998 Totline® Publications

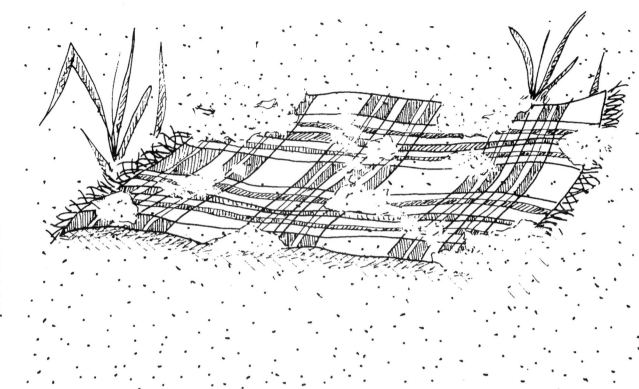

Sand on the blanket. 9

Sand on the shovel. 11

10 **Sand on the bear.**

12 **Sand everywhere!**

Totline® Publications

Teacher Books

BEST OF TOTLINE® SERIES
Totline Magazine's best ideas.
Best of Totline
Best of Totline Parent Flyers

BUSY BEES SERIES
Seasonal ideas for twos and threes.
Busy Bees—Fall
Busy Bees—Winter
Busy Bees—Spring
Busy Bees—Summer

CELEBRATIONS SERIES
Early learning through celebrations.
Small World Celebrations
Special Day Celebrations
Great Big Holiday Celebrations
Celebrating Likes and Differences

EXPLORING SERIES
Versatile, hands-on learning.
Exploring Sand
Exploring Water
Exploring Wood

FOUR SEASONS
Active learning through the year.
Four Seasons—Art
Four Seasons—Math
Four Seasons—Movement
Four Seasons—Science

GREAT BIG THEMES SERIES
Giant units designed around a theme.
Space • Zoo • Circus

KINDERSTATION SERIES
Learning centers for learning with language, art, and math.
Calculation Station
Communication Station
Creation Station
Investigation Station

LEARNING & CARING ABOUT
Teach children about their world.
Our World • Our Town

MIX & MATCH PATTERNS
Simple patterns to save time!
Animal Patterns
Everyday Patterns
Holiday Patterns
Nature Patterns

1•2•3 SERIES
Open-ended learning.
1•2•3 Art
1•2•3 Blocks
1•2•3 Games
1•2•3 Colors

1•2•3 Puppets
1•2•3 Reading & Writing
1•2•3 Rhymes, Stories & Songs
1•2•3 Math
1•2•3 Science
1•2•3 Shapes

1001 SERIES
Super reference books.
1001 Teaching Props
1001 Teaching Tips
1001 Rhymes & Fingerplays

PIGGYBACK® SONG BOOKS
New lyrics sung to the tunes of childhood favorites!
Piggyback Songs
More Piggyback Songs
Piggyback Songs for Infants and Toddlers
Holiday Piggyback Songs
Animal Piggyback Songs
Piggyback Songs for School
Piggyback Songs to Sign
Spanish Piggyback Songs
More Piggyback Songs for School

PROBLEM SOLVING SAFARI
Teaching problem solving skills.
Problem Solving—Art
Problem Solving—Blocks
Problem Solving—Dramatic Play
Problem Solving—Manipulatives
Problem Solving—Outdoors
Problem Solving—Science

REPRODUCIBLE RHYMES
Make-and-take books for emergent readers.
Alphabet Rhymes
Object Rhymes

SNACKS SERIES
Nutrition combines with learning.
Super Snacks • Healthy Snacks
Teaching Snacks • Multicultural Snacks

TERRIFIC TIPS
Handy resources full of valuable tips.
Terrific Tips for Directors
Terrific Tips for Toddler Teachers
Terrific Tips for Preschool Teachers

THEME-A-SAURUS® SERIES
Classroom-tested, instant themes.
Theme-A-Saurus
Theme-A-Saurus II
Toddler Theme-A-Saurus
Alphabet Theme-A-Saurus
Nursery Rhyme Theme-A-Saurus
Storytime Theme-A-Saurus
Multisensory Theme-A-Saurus

TODDLER SERIES
Great for working with 18 mos–3 yrs.
Playtime Props for Toddlers
Toddler Art

Tot-Mobiles
Unique sets of die-cut mobiles for punching out and easy assembly.
Animals & Toys
Beginning Concepts
Four Seasons

Puzzles & Posters

PUZZLES
Kids Celebrate the Alphabet
Kids Celebrate Numbers
African Adventure
Underwater Adventure
Bear Hugs 4-in-1 Puzzle Set
Busy Bees 4-in-1 Puzzle Set

POSTERS
We Work and Play Together
Bear Hugs Health Posters
Busy Bees Area Posters
Reminder Posters

Parent Books

A YEAR OF FUN SERIES
Age-specific books for parenting.
Just for Babies
Just for Ones
Just for Twos
Just for Threes
Just for Fours
Just for Fives

BEGINNING FUN WITH ART
Introduce your child to art fun.
Craft Sticks • Crayons • Felt
Glue • Paint • Paper Shapes
Modeling Dough • Tissue Paper
Scissors • Rubber Stamps
Stickers • Yarn

BEGINNING FUN WITH SCIENCE
Spark your child's interest in science.
Bugs & Butterflies • Plants & Flowers
Magnets • Rainbows & Colors
Sand & Shells • Water & Bubbles

KIDS CELEBRATE SERIES
Delightful stories with related activity ideas, snacks, and songs.
Kids Celebrate the Alphabet
Kids Celebrate Numbers

LEARN WITH PIGGYBACK® SONGS
Captivating music with age-appropriate themes help children learn.
Songs & Games for Babies
Songs & Games for Toddlers
Songs & Games for Threes
Songs & Games for Fours
Sing a Song of Letters
Sing a Song of Animals
Sing a Song of Colors
Sing a Song of Holidays
Sing a Song of Me
Sing a Song of Nature
Sing a Song of Numbers

LEARN WITH STICKERS
Beginning workbook and first reader with 100-plus stickers.
Balloons • Birds • Bows • Bugs
Butterflies • Buttons • Eggs • Flags
Flowers • Hearts • Leaves • Mittens

LEARNING EVERYWHERE
Discover teaching opportunities everywhere you go.
Teaching House
Teaching Trips
Teaching Town

PLAY AND LEARN
Activities for learning through play the Totline way.
Blocks • Instruments • Kitchen
Gadgets • Paper • Puppets • Puzzles

SEEDS FOR SUCCESS
Ideas to help children develop essential life skills for future success.
Growing Creative Kids
Growing Happy Kids
Growing Responsible Kids
Growing Thinking Kids

TIME TO LEARN
Ideas for hands-on learning.
Colors • Letters • Measuring
Numbers • Science • Shapes
Matching and Sorting • New Words
Cutting and Pasting
Drawing and Writing • Listening
Taking Care of Myself

Puppet Pals
These instant puppets fit on craft sticks, pencils or straws for language props, rewards, and more!
Children's Favorites • The Three Bears
Nursery Rhymes • Old MacDonald
More Nursery Rhymes • Three Little
Pigs • Three Billy Goats Gruff
Little Red Riding Hood